WEEKEND

SIMPLE,
MODERN
KNITS

12 designs by JEN GEIGLEY

PHOTOGRAPHY by JOELLE BLANCHARD, JOEY LEAMING and GEOF FISCHER

Design & Pattern Writing | Jen Geigley
Photography | Joelle Blanchard, Joey Leaming, Geof Fischer
Design, Layout & Illustrations | Jen Geigley
Technical Editing | Stefanie Goodwin-Ritter
Models | Joelle Blanchard, Geof Fischer, Lotus Geigley
Location | Lovejoy Building, Des Moines, Iowa

WEEKEND: Simple, Modern Knits

Wholesale Ordering Information
Deep South Fibers
www.deepsouthfibers.com

Library of Congress Control Number: 2015913493
ISBN: 978-0-9965805-0-2 hardback
ISBN: 978-0-9965805-1-9 paperback
ISBN: 978-0-9965805-2-6 ebook

((((((●
MOON PHASE PUBLICATIONS
www.MoonPhasePublications.com

CRA015000
Crafts & Hobbies | Needlework | Knitting

10 9 8 7 6 5 4 3 2 1

C O N T E N T S

TO MINNIE AND BETTY, MY CRAFTY GRANDMOTHERS. I HOPE THIS BOOK WOULD HAVE MADE YOU SMILE.

INTRODUCTION

Welcome to the weekend. Simple, modern knits you can live in on the weekend; knits you can create in a weekend. This collection brings wearability and simplicity together in a way that will appeal to brand-new and experienced knitters alike.

Knitting something warm to wear during a frigid Midwestern winter brings things back to basics for me. It slows me down and I like that. This collection of sweaters and accessories exudes comfort and ease. My mission is to create casual, contemporary, wearable knits that will serve as foundation pieces in anyone's wardrobe. Approachable patterns that aren't too complex, making knitters everywhere say, "I want to make that ... and I can make it this weekend."

I'm a minimalist at heart and I truly believe less is more and simple is good. To me, simple equals wearable. Simple equals doable. And there's no greater satisfaction than finishing a hand-knit piece, trying it on and falling in love with it. My goal as a knitter is to make go-to pieces that feel just right, like my favorite soft gray pullover from college. If you spend precious time knitting a garment, you want to love it and wear it over and over again. It's as simple as that. That, to me, is the definition of hand-knit success. And that's what I hope to share with you in this collection.

THE COLLECTION

ATMOSPHERE
page 98

FLOOR
page 100

DEBUT
page 102

FEEDBACK + DISTORTION
pages 106-108

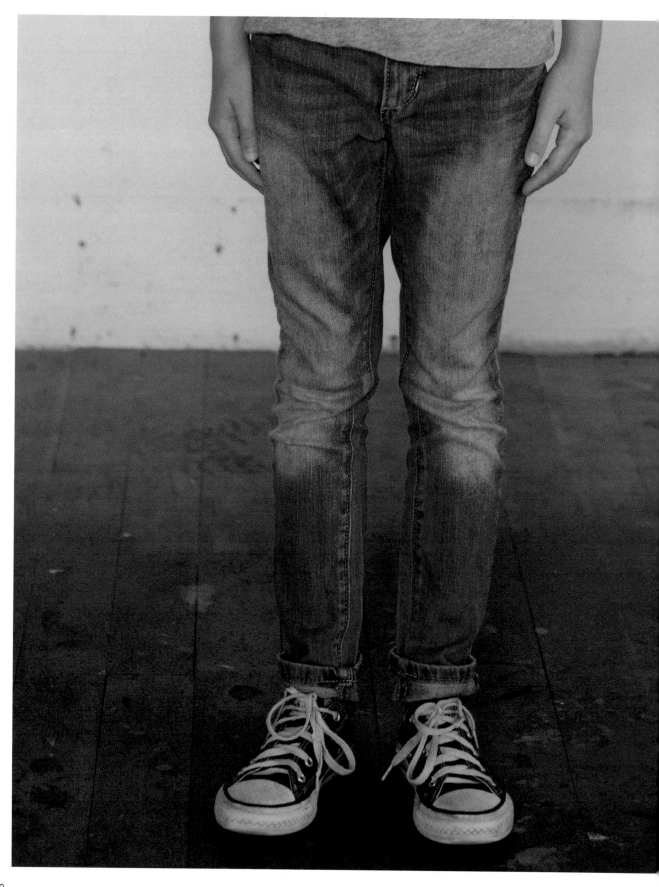

MINNIE
page 110

UNDONE
page 112

EVENFLOW
page 116

RETROGRADE
page 118

LITTLE EARTHQUAKES
page 120

VALHALLA
page 122

SLIVER
page 124

THE PATTERNS

ATMOSPHERE

DESIGN NOTES

This hat is all kinds of fun, and extremely quick to knit. Two strands of super bulky yarn are held together to knit this fashion-forward, super huge hat. Cover up your bed head or wear it out in the nastiest cold weather. Your friends will ask you to knit this hat for them and luckily, you can whip one up in less than an hour. The giant 5 inch diameter pom-pom is optional and this hat looks great with or without it, but heck, why not?

SIZES
One size

FINISHED MEASUREMENTS
19" circumference

YARN
Cascade Magnum in 'Koala Bear' (Super Bulky, 100% Peruvian Highland Wool; 123 yards per 250g skein) – 1 skein

NEEDLES
US 36 (20 mm) 16" circular needle
(or size needed to obtain gauge)
US 36 double-pointed needles

NOTIONS
Large stitch marker
Tape measure
Tapestry needle
Scissors

GAUGE
4 inches = 4 sts and 6 rows in St st on US 36 needles with yarn held double

TIP: When using extra large needles, an elastic hair tie makes a great stitch marker.

DIRECTIONS

Holding yarn double, use long tail cast on and size US 36 needle to CO 18 sts. Join to work in the round, taking care not to twist sts. PM to mark beginning of rnd.

K around for 7 rnds.

CROWN SHAPING (Switch to DPNs when necessary)

*K 4 sts, k2tog. Rep from * around – 15 sts rem.
Next rnd: k around.

*K 3 sts, k2tog. Rep from * around – 12 sts rem.
Next rnd: k around.

*K 2 sts, k2tog. Rep from * around – 9 sts rem.
Next rnd: k around.

FINISHING

Cut yarn, leaving a 6-8 in tail. Using tapestry needle, thread rem sts onto tail. Pull tight and secure. Use tapestry needle to weave in ends.

POM-POM (OPTIONAL)

Cut out two cardboard doughnuts 5 inches in diameter to make optional pom-pom. Sandwich a piece of yarn 8 inches long between the two layers. Cut a slit in both pieces of cardboard from outer edge to inner circle. Wind yarn over the doughnut, around and around, working the yarn through the center hole on each pass. Insert a scissors between the two layers of the form and cut the strands of pom-pom yarn where they cross over the outer edge of the circles. Pull up the center yarn tightly. Tie the center yarn in a tight knot. Fluff the pom-pom into shape and trim any stray ends. Use the center 8 inch piece of yarn to attach pom-pom to top of hat.

BLOCKING

Blocking this particular yarn/garment is usually not necessary. If blocking is needed, lay out garment and shape to desired shape and dimensions. Gently spritz with water in a spray bottle until damp, but not soaking wet. Allow to dry completely.

FLOOR

DESIGN NOTES

Wrap yourself up in Floor, an impressive extra long scarf. Floor is for the coldest of days or for whenever you feel like making a big statement. Let this scarf hang down to the ground, or wrap it around your neck repeatedly until you achieve ultimate coziness. This design is unisex and perfect for the beginner knitter who would like to practice knitting and purling. **Note: Slip the first stitch knitwise on each row to create nice, neat edges.**

SIZES
One size

FINISHED MEASUREMENTS
6¼ x 135 inches

YARN
Rowan Big Wool in 'Glum' (Super Bulky; 100% merino wool; 87 yards per 100g skein) – 5 balls

NEEDLES
US 15 (10 mm) needles
(or size needed to obtain gauge)

NOTIONS
Tape measure
Tapestry needle
Scissors

GAUGE
4 inches = 8 sts and 13 rows in seed st on US 15 needles

DIRECTIONS

Using long-tail method, CO 13 sts.

Row 1: Sl 1 kw, * p1, k1; rep from * across row.

Rep this row until piece measures 135 inches from CO edge.

BO in pattern, loosely. Break yarn.

FINISHING
Using tapestry needle, weave in ends.

BLOCKING
Lay out garment and shape to desired shape and dimensions. Spritz with cool water in a spray bottle until damp, but not soaking wet. Allow to dry completely.

DEBUT

DESIGN NOTES

Debut is a luxuriously fantastic kimono, knitted flat in super bulky yarn. Whether you are lounging about at home or heading out for a night on the town, this kimono will make you feel like the extraordinary knitting hero that you are. At home, Debut can be your fancy robe of leisure. Cozy up in it like it's a blanket – a blanket of fashion. Impress your friends when you wear it out to brunch. Layer it over a little black dress when you head out for your evening escapades and stay warm while looking fabulous. This piece is one of my favorite garments in this collection and it's named after my favorite Björk album. (I bet Björk would wear a giant hand-knit kimono.)

SIZES
One size

FINISHED MEASUREMENTS
Bust – 42 inches
Length (shoulder to bottom edge) – 24 inches
Sleeves – 12 inches

YARN
Cascade Magnum (Super Bulky; 100% Peruvian Highland Wool; 123 yards per 250g skein) – 4 skeins

NEEDLES
US 19 (15 mm) 29" circular needles
(or size needed to obtain gauge)

NOTIONS
Tape measure
Tapestry needle
Scissors

GAUGE
4 inches = 6 sts and 9 rows in St st on US 19 (15 mm) needles

STITCHES
1x1 Rib:
Row 1 (RS): *K1, p1, rep from * to end of row.
Row 2 (WS): *P1, k1, rep from * to end of row.

DIRECTIONS

BACK
Using long tail method, CO 36 sts.
Work in 1x1 rib for 4 rows.
Beg working in St st until piece measures 24 inches from CO edge.
BO.

FRONT (MAKE 2)
Using long tail method, CO 14 sts.
Work in 1x1 rib for 4 rows.
Beg working in St st until piece measures 24 inches from CO edge.
BO.

SLEEVE (MAKE 2)
Using long tail method, CO 46 sts.
Work in 1x1 rib for 4 rows.
Beg working in St st until piece measures 12 inches from CO edge.
BO.

SEAMING (See page 132)
Use tapestry needle and yarn tails to seam. See schematics.
1. Fold each sleeve in half and seam along bottom edge.
2. Seam shoulders using shoulder seam stitch.
3. Pin sleeves to body and seam sleeves to front pieces and back, leaving the bottom 6 inches of each sleeve open and un-seamed.
4. Sew side seams using mattress stitch.

NECK BAND (See page 132)
With RS facing, pick up and knit 40 sts along right front edge, 17 sts across back of neck and 40 sts along left front edge. (97 sts)

Next row: Sl 1, work in 1x1 rib for 4 rows, slipping first st on each row. BO very loosely in pattern.

FINISHING
Using tapestry needle, weave in ends.

BLOCKING
Blocking this particular yarn/garment is usually not necessary. If blocking is needed, lay out garment and shape to desired shape and dimensions. Gently spritz with water in a spray bottle until damp, but not soaking wet. Allow to dry completely.

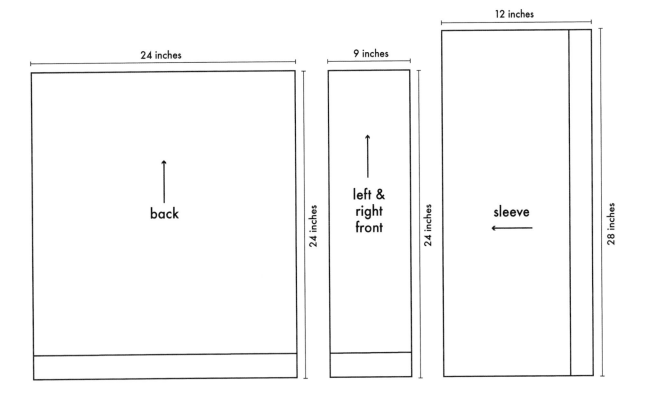

24 inches

back

24 inches

9 inches

left & right front

24 inches

12 inches

sleeve

28 inches

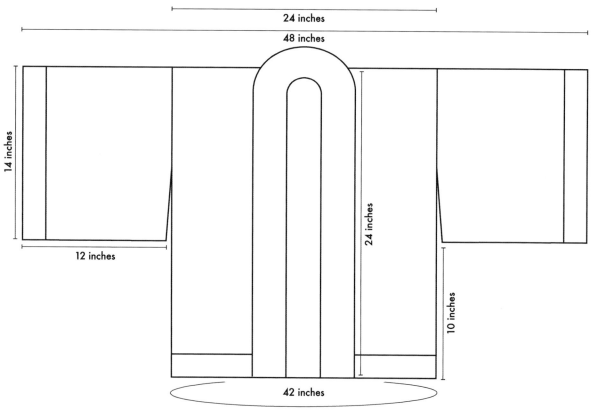

24 inches

48 inches

14 inches

12 inches

24 inches

10 inches

42 inches

DESIGN NOTES

Cowls are cool when they're worn by a kid. Knit up this simple, cozy accessory for any child in your life. Cowls make a lot of sense for kids since they're easy to throw on and unlike a scarf, there are no tails to fuss over. The duplicate stitch detail in this design adds a little bit of edginess. If you've never attempted this technique before, now is the perfect time to give it a try.

SIZES
One Size – Child

FINISHED MEASUREMENTS
10 x 9 inches (laid flat)

YARN
Wool and the Gang Crazy Sexy Wool in 'Khaki Green' (Super Bulky, 100% Peruvian wool; 87 yards per 200 g ball) – 1 ball

Wool and the Gang Crazy Sexy Wool in 'Eagle Grey' – scrap piece, 8–12" for duplicate stitch

NEEDLES
US 17 (13 mm) 16" circular needles (or size needed to obtain gauge)
US 17 (13 mm) DPNs

NOTIONS
Stitch marker
Tape measure
Tapestry needle
Scissors

GAUGE
4 inches = 6 sts and 10 rows in St st on US 17 (13 mm) needles

TIP: If you're not accustomed to using super bulky yarn, take care not to stab your yarn with the points of your needle – it can cause the yarn to get fuzzy. Knit slowly and your stitches will stay smooth and clean.

DIRECTIONS

Using long tail cast on and US 17 circular needle, CO 36 sts.

Join and PM, taking care not to twist sts.

*K1, p1 (single rib), rep from * around. Rep for 2 rnds.

K around (st st) until piece measures 7¼ inches from CO edge.

*K1, p1 (single rib), rep from * around. Rep for 1 rnd.

BO in pattern, loosely. Break yarn.

FINISHING

Cut yarn, leaving a 6-8 in tail. Using tapestry needle, weave in ends.

EMBROIDERY DETAIL – DUPLICATE STITCH

Thread scrap piece of yarn in contrasting color onto tapestry needle and decide where you want your stitching to begin. Bring the point of the tapestry needle up through the point of the V in the first stitch you want to duplicate; pull the yarn through, leaving a few inches of yarn at the back of the work to weave in later. Working from right to left, slide needle behind the V of the stitch above the stitch you are working on. Gently pull the yarn through. Next, insert the needle back through the point of the V where you started. Pull through. You have now finished one duplicate stitch. Skipping the stitch directly above the stitch you just covered, insert the needle up through point of the V in the next stitch you want to duplicate. Repeat these steps to make three decorative duplicate stitches in your contrast color. Try to keep your tension the same as the original stitches in the cowl. When finished, weave in loose ends on wrong side of cowl, secure and cut ends.

BLOCKING

Blocking this particular yarn/garment is usually not necessary. If blocking is needed, lay out garment and shape to desired shape and dimensions. Gently spritz with water in a spray bottle until damp, but not soaking wet. Allow to dry completely.

DISTORTION

DESIGN NOTES

Knitting this hat is a piece of cake and takes no time at all. Distortion makes the perfect hat for beginner knitters learning to knit in the round, and the duplicate stitch detail is an easy way to try out new color combinations and make this project your own. Knit one (or five) of these super warm kids' hats this weekend.

SIZES
One Size – Child

FINISHED MEASUREMENTS
16 inches circumference

YARN
Wool and the Gang Crazy Sexy Wool in 'Khaki Green' (Super Bulky, 100% Peruvian wool; 87 yards per 200 g ball) – 1 ball

Wool and the Gang Crazy Sexy Wool in 'Eagle Grey' – scrap piece, 8-12" for duplicate stitch

NEEDLES
US 17 (13 mm) 16" circular needles (or size needed to obtain gauge)
US 17 (13 mm) DPNs

NOTIONS
Stitch marker
Tape measure
Tapestry needle
Scissors

GAUGE
4 inches = 6 sts and 10 rows in St st on US 17 (13 mm) needles

DIRECTIONS

Using long tail cast on and US 17 circular needle, CO 24 sts.

Join and PM, taking care not to twist sts.

*K1, p1 (single rib), rep from * around. Rep for 3 rnds.

K around (st st) until piece measures 7 inches from CO edge.

CROWN SHAPING (Switch to DPNs when necessary)

Decrease Rnd 1: *K 4 sts, k2tog. Rep from * around.
20 sts rem.

K around.
Decrease Rnd 2: *K 3 sts, k2tog. Rep from * around.
16 sts rem.

K around.

Decrease Rnd 3: *K 2 sts, k2tog. Rep from * around.
12 sts rem.

K around.

FINISHING
Cut yarn, leaving a 6-8 in tail. Using tapestry needle, thread rem sts onto tail. Pull tight and secure, weave in ends.

EMBROIDERY DETAIL – DUPLICATE STITCH
Thread scrap piece of yarn in contrasting color onto tapestry needle and decide where you want your stitching to begin. Bring the point of the tapestry needle up through the point of the V in the first stitch you want to duplicate; pull the yarn through, leaving a few inches of yarn at the back of the work to weave in later. Working from right to left, slide needle behind the V of the stitch above the stitch you are working on. Gently pull the yarn through. Next, insert the needle back through the point of the V where you started. Pull through. You have now finished one duplicate stitch. Skipping the stitch directly above the stitch you just covered, insert the needle through point of the V in the next stitch you want to duplicate. Repeat these steps to make three decorative duplicate stitches in your contrast color. Try to keep your tension the same as the stitches in the hat. When finished, weave in loose ends on wrong side of hat, secure and cut ends.

BLOCKING
Blocking this particular yarn/garment is usually not necessary. If blocking is needed, lay out garment and shape to desired shape and dimensions. Gently spritz with water in a spray bottle until damp, but not soaking wet. Allow to dry completely.

MINNIE

DESIGN NOTES

Minnie is a hoodie/scarf, worked flat and then seamed. It's the best of both worlds. Minnie is named after my grandmother, who was a crafter of all sorts and a huge inspiration to me growing up. This hooded scarf reminds me of the headscarves she'd wear to protect her hair from the wind. You can do this too, my friends. Wear Minnie with the hood up or down, depending on how cold your ears (and face) are. Wrap up the ends of the scarf for layered warmth or tie them in a knot.

SIZES
One size
Scarf – 5 x 65 inches
Hood – 10¼ x 9 inches (flat)

FINISHED MEASUREMENTS
10 x 9 inches (laid flat)

YARN
Rowan Big Wool in 'Smoky' (Super Bulky; 100% merino wool; 87 yards per 100g skein) – 2.5 balls

NEEDLES
US 11 (8 mm) needles (or size needed to obtain gauge)
US 10 (6 mm) needle (for 3 needle bind off)

NOTIONS
Tape measure
Tapestry needle
Scissors

GAUGE
Scarf: 4 inches = 9 sts and 13 rows in seed st on US 11 needles
Hood: 4 inches = 8½ sts and 12 rows in St st on US 11 needles

STITCHES
Seed Stitch:
Row 1 (RS): *k1, p1, rep from * to end of row.
Row 2 (WS): *p1, k1, rep from * to end of row.

DIRECTIONS

SCARF
CO 10 sts.
Work in seed stitch until piece measures 65 in from CO edge.

BO and weave in ends.

HOOD
CO 44 sts.
Rows 1–3: Work seed stitch across all sts.
Row 4 (RS): P1, k1, p1, k to last 3 sts, k1, p1, k1.
Row 5 (WS): K1, p1, k1, p to last 3 sts, p1, k1, p1.
Rep rows 4 and 5 until piece measures 9 in from CO edge, ending with row 5.

Next row:
P1, k1, p1, k 19 sts. (Each needle should be holding half of the sts.)

With right sides facing, use smaller needle to work a 3-needle BO. (See page 132.)

FINISHING
Fold scarf in half and match middle point to seam on hood. Pin together with locking stitch markers or pins. Using tapestry needle, seam hood to scarf and weave in ends.

BLOCKING
Lay out garment and shape to desired shape and dimensions. Spritz with cool water in a spray bottle until damp, but not soaking wet. Allow to dry completely.

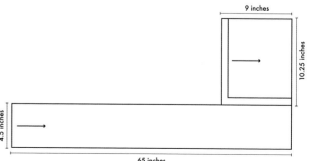

UNDONE

DESIGN NOTES

Undone is bound to be a favorite pullover, earning a special spot in your closet. Soft and cozy, this everyday stockinette sweater is perfect for leisurely days at home or coffee dates with friends. Undone will get you through whatever your weekend throws at you. Knit in the round from the top down, this simple raglan has two side zippers at the bottom that not only look cool, but also add to the comfort and ease of wearing this classic pullover. (And yes, it's named after Weezer's "The Sweater Song.")

SIZES

XS (S, M, L, 1X, 2X, 3X)

TO FIT BUST

32 (36, 40, 44, 48, 52, 56) inches

FINISHED BUST MEASUREMENTS

34 (38, 42, 46, 50, 54, 58) inches

YARN

Spud and Chloe Outer in 'Rhino' (Super Bulky; superwash 65% wool/35% organic cotton; 60 yards per 100g hank)

9 (10, 10, 11, 13, 15, 17) hanks
540 (600, 600, 660, 780, 900, 1020) yards

NEEDLES

US 11 (7 mm) 24 in circular needles; US 11 (7 mm) DPNs
US 10 (6.5 mm) 24 in circular needles; US 10 (6.5 mm) DPNs (or size needed to obtain gauge)

NOTIONS

Stitch markers (4 in one color, 1 in contrast color)
Two 5 inch separating zippers (in color of your choice)
Sewing thread that matches yarn color
Sewing needle
Straight pins
Tape measure
Tapestry needle
Scissors

GAUGE

4 inches = 10 sts and 12 rows in St st on larger needles

ABBREVIATIONS

kfb - **knit into the front and back** of the same stitch (one stitch increased)
LLI - **left lifted increase:** use LH needle to pick up stitch below st just knitted, then knit into it (one stitch increased)
RLI - **right lifted increase:** knit into back loop of st below next st (one stitch increased)

DIRECTIONS

Using long-tail method and larger needles, CO 35 (35, 38, 38, 41, 41, 44) sts. Do not join; work flat.

SET-UP ROW

K2, pm, k6 (6, 7, 7, 8, 8, 9) sts, pm, k19 (19, 20, 20, 21, 21, 22) sts, pm, k6 (6, 7, 7, 8, 8, 9) sts, pm, k2.
Next Row: P across.

RAGLAN INCREASES

Next Row (inc): Kfb, RLI, sm, k1, LLI, *k to 1 st before marker, RLI, sm, k1, LLI; repeat from * 2 more times, kfb. 10 sts increased – 45 (45, 48, 48, 51, 51, 54) sts.
Next Row: P across.

Next Row (inc): Kfb, *k to 1 st before marker, RLI, sm, k1, LLI; repeat from * 3 more times, k to last st, kfb. 10 sts increased.
Next Row: P across.
Repeat last 2 rows 2 more times. 75 (75, 78, 78, 81, 81, 84) sts.

CO 10 (10, 11, 13, 13, 14, 15) sts, join to work in the round, taking care not to twist sts. PM in contrasting color to mark beginning of round. 85 (85, 89, 91, 94, 95, 99) sts.

Next Rnd (inc): *K to 1 st before marker, RLI, sm, k1, LLI; repeat from * 3 times more, k to end. 8 sts increased.
Next Rnd: K around.
Repeat last 2 rows 6 (8, 10, 12, 12, 13, 14) more times. 141 (157, 177, 195, 198, 207, 219) sts.

Size S, M, L, 1x only:

Next Rnd: Incr back only. K to first marker, sm, k to next m, sm, k1, LLI, to 1 st before marker, RLI, sm, k to end. 2 sts increased – (159, 179, 197, 200) sts.
Next Rnd: K around.

Size, 1X, 2X and 3X only:

Next Rnd: Increase body only. *K to 1 st before marker, RLI, sm, k to m, sm, k1, LLI; rep from * once more, k to end. 4 sts increased – (204, 211, 223) sts.
Next Rnd: K around.

Size 1X, 2X and 3X only:

Next Rnd: Increase body only. *K to 1 st before marker, RLI, sm, k to m, sm, k1, LLI; rep from * once more, k to end. 4 sts increased – (208, 215, 227) sts.

Size 2X and 3X only:

Next Rnd: Increase body only. *K to 1 st before marker, RLI, sm, k to m, sm, k1, LLI; rep from * once more, k to end. 4 sts increased.

Repeat this rnd (1, 2) more time. (223, 239) sts.

141 (159, 179, 197, 208, 215, 239) sts. **(See chart below.)**

STITCH COUNTS

SIZES	XS	S	M	L	1X	2X	3X
FRONT	44	48	53	59	63	70	75
SLEEVE	28	32	37	41	42	44	47
BACK	41	47	52	56	61	65	70
SLEEVE	28	32	37	41	42	44	47
TOTAL	141	159	179	197	208	215	239

DIVIDE BODY AND SLEEVES

From the beginning of your rnd, k to your first marker. Remove marker. Place next 28 (32, 37, 41, 42, 44, 47) sts on holder. (First sleeve.) Pick up your working yarn and work across the back sts until third marker. Remove marker. Place next 28 (32, 37, 41, 42, 44, 47) sts on holder. Leave last marker on needle. (Second sleeve.) All sts remaining on your needle will make up the body of your sweater.

Work in St st until body of sweater measures 9 (9½, 10, 10½, 11, 11½, 12) inches from underarm.

85 (95, 105, 115, 124, 135, 145) sts.

BOTTOM SECTIONS, FRONT AND BACK

Note: Each section is worked flat; you may wish to move the unworked portion of stitches to scrap yarn or a stitch holder while working the first half.

Next Rnd: K44 (48, 53, 59, 63, 70, 75) sts, PM. K to beg of rnd marker (next marker).

Next Row: (Back) Turn, p to marker. Slipping first st of each row, work this section back and forth in St st until piece

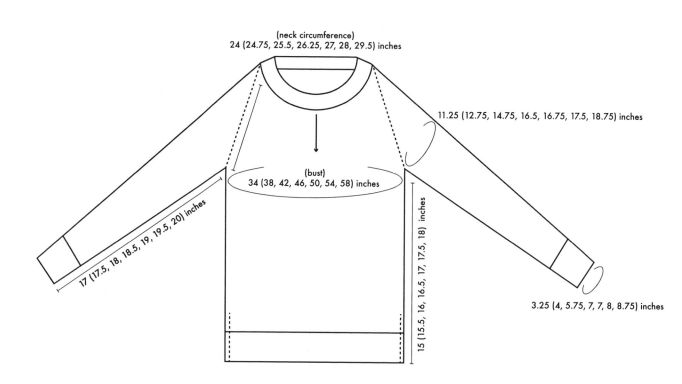

(neck circumference)
24 (24.75, 25.5, 26.25, 27, 28, 29.5) inches

11.25 (12.75, 14.75, 16.5, 16.75, 17.5, 18.75) inches

(bust)
34 (38, 42, 46, 50, 54, 58) inches

17 (17.5, 18, 18.5, 19, 19.5, 20) inches

15 (15.5, 16, 16.5, 17, 17.5, 18) inches

3.25 (4, 5.75, 7, 7, 8, 8.75) inches

measures 3 inches from where you began working flat.
Next Row: Switch to smaller needle. Work in 1x1 rib (k1, p1) for 3 inches – if you have an odd number of sts for your size, p2tog at the end of the first row.
BO knitwise, loosely. Break yarn.
Join yarn and repeat for Front section on reserved K44 (48, 53, 59, 63, 70, 75) sts.

SLEEVES

Starting at underarm and using larger needles, transfer one set of reserved sleeve stitches from holder to needles. PM at underarm to mark beginning of rnd.

Join new end of working yarn (leaving a tail for finishing) and work in St st, decreasing 1 st on each side of marker every 4 (4, 4, 4, 4, 4, 4) rnds.

Continue in this manner until sleeve measures 14 (14½, 15, 15½, 16, 16½, 17) inches from underarm – 8 (10, 15, 19, 18, 20, 23) sts rem. Adjust number of sts by decreasing 1 st if needed to obtain an even number of sts for ribbed cuff – 8 (10, 14, 18, 18, 20, 22) sts rem.

CUFF

Next Rnd: Switch to smaller needles. Work in 1x1 rib (k1, p1) for 3 inches.
BO in pattern, loosely. Break yarn.

Repeat for remaining sleeve.

NECK

Working in the round and starting at the left back raglan, pick up and k60 (62, 64, 66, 68, 70, 74) sts evenly around neck using smaller needles. (Tip: Point needle into neck stitches from outside to inside of sweater.)
Next Rnd: Work in 1x1 rib (k1, p1) for 1½ inches.
BO in pattern, loosely. Break yarn.

FINISHING

Use tapestry needle and yarn tail at underarm to close and neaten gap under each arm. Weave in all ends.

BLOCKING

Lay out garment and shape to desired shape and dimensions. Spritz with cool water in a spray bottle until damp, but not soaking wet. Allow to dry completely.

ZIPPERS

Add one 5 inch separating zipper to each side of the bottom of sweater after blocking.

ZIPPER SEWING DIRECTIONS

With zipper closed and the RS of your knitting facing up, pin right side of zipper to sweater BO edge. Cover as much of the fabric zipper flaps with your knitting as possible, but keep knitted edge far enough from zipper that it won't snag. Keep the zipper and the knitted edge flat and relaxed as you pin– not too tight, but also not loose enough to pucker.

With the RS of sweater facing you, sew the zipper to the sweater in a straight line using matching thread. Make small stitches. Stitch as close to the zipper as you can, taking care to keep your stitches as invisible as possible.

Pin the second side of zipper to the second BO edge. Unzip the zipper if you'd like.

Repeat sewing instructions above.

Unzip the zipper (if you haven't already) and turn sweater inside out. Sew outer edges of zipper flaps (using blind stitch or slip stitch) to the sweater, taking care to keep stitches as invisible as possible. Sew along a column of the stitches in your knitting to keep the zipper straight.

Fold up ends of the zipper (if they stick out) and tack down.

EVENFLOW

DESIGN NOTES

Evenflow is perhaps the most striking accessory you'll ever knit, and you can finish it in an evening. No needles are necessary, because you'll be using your arms to knit this scarf out of wool roving. Slow and steady is the way to go, and in no time you'll have a gigantic, chunky accessory that makes an impact. Oversized is always in fashion, and knitting with your arms gives this piece lots of flexibility and drape. If you've never attempted arm knitting before, you'll be thrilled with how fun and easy it is. Anyone can make Evenflow, and everyone will want you to show them how it's done.

SIZES
One size

FINISHED MEASUREMENTS
9 x 110 inches (may vary)

YARN
2 pounds (907 gr) **Ashland Bay Merino Roving**

NEEDLES
Your arms

NOTIONS
Scissors

GAUGE
Scarf: 3 inches = 1 st

DIRECTIONS

Using left hand and long-tail method, CO 3 sts onto your right arm.

Row 1: With right hand, grab working yarn and sl first st on wrist off your hand. Pull working yarn through the st, making a loop. Slide your left hand through the loop from back to front. Rep for next 2 sts, except slide your left wrist through the loop from front to back.

Row 2: With left hand, grab working yarn and sl first st on wrist off your hand. Pull working yarn through the st, making a loop. Slide your right hand through the loop from back to front. Rep for next 2 sts, except slide your right wrist through the loop from front to back.

Rep Rows 1 & 2 until your have used all but 12" of roving.

To BO, work sts as above until you have 2 sts on your arm. Drop working yarn. Using fingers, pick up the fist st you knit on your arm and pull that st over the last st you knit. Rep once more; 1 st rem. Thread tail through last st and pull taught.

FINISHING
Using your fingers, tuck in any stray ends.

VIDEO
For additional help with learning how to arm knit, check out Wool and the Gang's DIY Arm Knitting Tutorial on YouTube. https://www.youtube.com/watch?v=Fh5x40Y2Bd0

RETROGRADE

DESIGN NOTES

I was knitting with friends when the idea for this scarf came about. I wanted to make a super long scarf with two sections that met and grew larger in the middle, like a cowl in the middle of a scarf. My friend said 'What if it went out like this, and then in like this!?' A couple of sketches later, Retrograde was born. This unisex scarf is knit in a reversible twin rib that looks great on both sides, and the extra long length adds a little drama to your ensemble. Wear this scarf all wrapped up in layers or throw it on and let the ends hang down. Either way, you're going to be warm and stylish. **Note: Slip the first stitch knitwise on each row to create nice, neat edges.**

SIZES
One size

FINISHED MEASUREMENTS
8 x 105 inches

YARN
Rowan Big Wool in 'Concrete' (Super Bulky; 100% merino wool; 87 yards per 100g skein) – 4 balls

NEEDLES
US 15 (10 mm) needles (or size needed to obtain gauge)

NOTIONS
Tape measure
Tapestry needle
Scissors

GAUGE
4 inches = 8 sts and 10 rows in twin rib st on US 15 needles

DIRECTIONS

SECTION 1
Using long-tail method, CO 15 sts.

Row 1: (RS) Sl 1 kw, p2, k3, *p3, k3; rep from * to last 3 sts, p3.

Row 2: (WS) Sl 1 kw, p1, *k1, p1; rep from * to last st, k1.

Rep rows 1 and 2 until piece measures 40 inches from CO edge.

SECTION 2
Ending after row 2, CO 9 sts at beg of next RS row. (24 sts)

Row 3 (RS): Sl 1 kw, k2, p3, *k3, p3; rep from * across row.

Row 4 (WS): Sl 1 kw, p1,*k1, p1; rep from * across row.

Rep rows 3 and 4 until section measures 25 inches.

SECTION 3
Ending after Row 3, BO 9 sts in pattern at beg of next WS row. (15 sts)

Row 5 (WS): *k1, p1; rep from * across row.

Row 6 (RS): Sl 1 kw, k2, p3, *k3, p3; rep from * to last 3 sts, k3.

Row 7 (WS): Sl 1 kw, k1, *p1, k1; rep from * to last st, k1.

Rep rows 6 and 7 until section measures 40 inches.

BO in pattern, loosely. Break yarn.

FINISHING
Using tapestry needle, weave in ends.

BLOCKING
Lay out garment and shape to desired shape and dimensions. Spritz with cool water in a spray bottle until damp, but not soaking wet. Allow to dry completely.

LITTLE EARTHQUAKES

DESIGN NOTES

I have been yearning to knit a gigantic neck tube that I could also wear as a hood for quite some time. Little Earthquakes is the giant, super bulky, unisex cowl of my dreams. Knit one up and you will see how fun this piece can be. It looks great no matter how you wear it, and it's ever-so-practical for keeping warm in cold climates. Wear it loosely around your neck and you will be impressed with how much warmer you will feel. Pull it up over your head and you've got an instant, giant hood to keep your ears and face warm. You will be so glad you added this versatile accessory to your cold-weather wardrobe, and you can knit one this weekend.

SIZES
One size

FINISHED MEASUREMENTS
20 x 22 inches (flat)

YARN
Wool and the Gang Crazy Sexy Wool in 'Eagle Grey' (Super Bulky, 100% Peruvian wool; 87 yards per 200 g ball) – 2 balls

NEEDLES
US 19 (15 mm) circular needles. 29" length (or size needed to obtain gauge)

NOTIONS
Stitch marker
Tapestry needle
Scissors

GAUGE
4 inches = 4 sts and 7 rows in 2x2 rib on US 19 (15 mm) needles

DIRECTIONS

Using long tail cast-on and US 19 circular needle, CO 48 sts. Join to work in the round, taking care not to twist sts. PM to mark beginning of rnd.

*K3, p3, rep from * for 4 rnds.

Next row: *K2, p2, rep from * until piece measures 10 inches from CO edge.

Next row: *P2, k2, rep from * until piece measures 18 inches from CO edge.

Next row: *K3, p3, rep from * for 3 rnds.

BO in pattern, loosely. Break yarn.

FINISHING

Cut yarn, leaving a 6-8 in tail. Using tapestry needle, weave in ends.

BLOCKING

Blocking this particular yarn/garment is usually not necessary. If blocking is needed, lay out garment and shape to desired shape and dimensions. Gently spritz with water in a spray bottle until damp, but not soaking wet. Allow to dry completely.

VALHALLA

DESIGN NOTES

This basic cowl is anything but. Knit as a tube in the round, the super bulky yarn creates a slouchy fabric that transforms into the very best shapes for any outfit you wear and whatever level of warmth you crave. Bunch it up and wear it indoors with a flannel shirt. On a chilly fall evening, throw it on over a leather jacket. Tuck it into your wool coat and bury your nose deep inside to beat the chill of blustery, snowy days. Simple equals functional and I promise that you will be wearing Valhalla nonstop this season and for years to come.

SIZES
One size

FINISHED MEASUREMENTS
Circumference – 38 inches
Width – 10 inches

YARN
Rowan Big Wool in 'Glum' (Super Bulky; 100% merino wool; 87 yards per 100g skein) – 3 balls

NEEDLES
US 15 (10 mm) 32" circular needles
(or size needed to obtain gauge)

NOTIONS
Tape measure
Tapestry needle
Stitch Marker
Scissors

GAUGE
4 inches = 8 sts and 11 rows in St st on US 15 needles

DIRECTIONS

VERSION 1 – WITH SEAM (SHOWN)
Using long tail cast on, CO 45 sts. Join to work in the round, taking care not to twist sts. PM to mark beginning of round.

K around (St st) until piece measures 38 inches from CO edge, unstretched.

BO loosely, break yarn.

FINISHING
Seam the CO and BO edges together. Using tapestry needle, weave in ends.

VERSION 2 – SEAMLESS (See page 132)
Using provisional cast on, CO 45 sts. Join to work in the round, taking care not to twist sts. PM to mark beginning of round.

K around (St st) until piece measures 38 inches from CO edge, unstretched.

Next row: Remove waste yarn from your provisional CO edge and pick up 'live' stitches.

FINISHING (See page 132)
Use the kitchener stitch to seamlessly graft ends together. Using tapestry needle, weave in ends.

BLOCKING
Lay out garment and shape to desired shape and dimensions listed above. Spritz with cool water in a spray bottle until damp, but not soaking wet. Allow to dry completely.

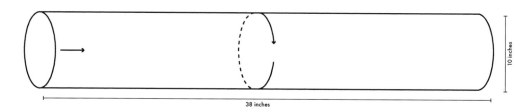

38 inches

10 inches

SLIVER

DESIGN NOTES

Sliver is the basic hat everyone needs, and that's why it's been designed in five sizes – XS through XL. Knit in the round, Sliver is unisex and can be worn by kids, too. A yarn forward and dropped stitches create a 'run' in the hat. Sliver is named after one of my favorite Nirvana songs, and the first test sample of this hat was knit in olive green, inspired by Kurt Cobain's memorable ragged green cardigan.

SIZES

Sizes: XS (S, M, L, XL)

FINISHED MEASUREMENTS

XS – 15" circumference
S – 17" circumference
M – 19½" circumference
L – 22" circumference
XL – 25" circumference

YARN

Wool and the Gang Crazy Sexy Wool in 'Eagle Gray' (Super Bulky, 100% Peruvian wool; 87 yards per 200 g ball) – 1 ball (Also shown in 'Big Bird Yellow')

NEEDLES

US 15 (10 mm) 16" circular needles
(or size needed to obtain gauge)
US 15 (10 mm) double pointed needles

NOTIONS

2 stitch markers (in contrasting colors)
Tapestry needle
Tape measure
Scissors

GAUGE

4 inches = 6½ sts and 10 rows in St st on US 15 (10 mm) needles

ABBREVIATIONS

DPN – double pointed needle
sl – slip
sm – slip marker
yfwd – bring working yarn to the front of your work between the two needles, then knit next stitch specified in pattern

DIRECTIONS

Using long tail cast on and US 15 circular needle, CO 24 (28, 32, 36, 40) sts.

Join and PM, taking care not to twist sts.

*K1, p1 (single rib), rep from * around. Rep for 4 rnds.

K around (st st) for 3 rnds.

Next rnd: K5, PM, yfwd, then k around (st st) for 10 (10, 12, 12, 14) rnds total, slipping the marker each time (marked st will be dropped later).

Next rnd: K to stitch marker and remove, drop the next st and unravel down to yfwd located just above ribbed section.

K around (st st) until piece measures 7 (7¼, 7½, 7¾, 8) inches from CO edge.

CROWN SHAPING (Switch to DPNs when necessary)

Decrease Rnd 1: *K 4 (5, 6, 7, 8) sts, k2tog. Rep from * around.
20 (24, 28, 32, 36) sts rem.

K around.

Decrease Rnd 2: *K 3 (4, 5, 6, 7) sts, k2tog. Rep from * around.
16 (20, 24, 28, 32) sts rem.

K around.

Decrease Rnd 3: *K 2 (3, 4, 5, 6) sts, k2tog. Rep from * around.
12 (16, 20, 24, 28) sts rem.

K around.

For size XS, proceed to Finishing. For all other sizes:

Decrease Rnd 4: *K – (2, 3, 4, 5) sts, k2tog. Rep from * around.
– (12, 16, 20, 24) sts rem.

K around.

For size S, proceed to Finishing. For all other sizes:

Decrease Rnd 5: *K – (–, 2, 3, 4) sts, k2tog. Rep from * around.

– (–, 12, 16, 20) sts rem.

K around.

For size M, proceed to Finishing. For all other sizes:

Decrease Rnd 6: *K – (–, –, 2, 3) sts, k2tog. Rep from * around.

– (–, –, 12, 16) sts rem.

K around.

For size L, proceed to Finishing. For size XL:

Decrease Rnd 7: *K – (–, –, –, 2) sts, k2tog. Rep from * around.

– (–, –, –, 12) sts rem.

K around.

FINISHING

Cut yarn, leaving a 6-8 in tail. Using tapestry needle, thread rem sts onto tail. Pull tight and secure, weave in ends.

BLOCKING

Blocking this particular yarn/garment is usually not necessary. If blocking is needed, lay out garment and shape to desired shape and dimensions. Gently spritz with water in a spray bottle until damp, but not soaking wet. Allow to dry completely.

RESOURCES

SOURCES

YARN

Cascade Yarns
813 Thomas Ave SW
Renton, WA 98057
(425) 970-4644
www.cascadeyarns.com

Rowan Yarns
Green Lane Mill
Holmfirth
West Yorkshire
England
HD9 2DX
www.knitrowan.com

Spud & Chloë
P.O. Box 88
Cedar, MN 55011
www.spudandchloe.com

Wool and the Gang
89a Shacklewell Lane
London, UK
E8 2EB
www.woolandthegang.com

NEEDLES & SUPPLIES

Knitter's Pride
www.knitterspride.com

Fringe Supply Co.
www.fringesupplyco.com

ABBREVIATIONS

beg beginning

BO bind off

CO cast on

cont continue

dec decrease

DPN double pointed needle

foll following

in inches

inc increase

k knit

k2tog knit 2 together

kfb knit into the front and back of the same stitch (one stitch increased)

kw knitwise

LLI left lifted increase: use left-hand needle to pick up stitch below stitch just knitted, then knit into it (one stitch increased)

mm millimeters

p purl

pm place marker

rem remaining

rep repeat

RLI right lifted increase: knit into back loop of stitch below next stitch (one stitch increased)

rnd(s) round(s)

RS right side

sl slip

sl 1 kw slip 1 knitwise

sm slip marker

st(s) stitch(es)

st st stockinette stitch

tog together

WS wrong side

yfwd yarn forward: bring working yarn to the front of your work between the two needles, then knit next stitch specified in pattern

SPECIAL TECHNIQUES

LONG TAIL CAST ON

Begin with a long tail, roughly three times the width of your finished piece of knitting. Leaving your estimated length of yarn for the long tail, make a slip knot. Place the slip knot on one needle and gently pull the yarn tails to tighten. Hold needle in your right hand with the tip of the needle pointing to the left. Using your left hand, grasp the two yarn ends below the slip knot. With your left thumb pressing against your left forefinger, move your thumb and forefinger through the space between the two strands. The long tail should be lying over your thumb and the working yarn over your forefinger. Spread your thumb and forefinger apart and lower the needle so that the yarn makes a V between the thumb and forefinger. Hold both tails tightly against your palm with your ring and pinky finger. With the needle in your right hand, pass the needle under the yarn around the thumb, over the top of the yarn around the forefinger, and back through the yarn around the thumb. Pull the thumb out from the yarn loop and pull gently on the yarn tails to tighten stitch. Repeat these steps until you have cast on the required number of stitches.

MATTRESS STITCH – VERTICAL

Lay pieces to be sewn flat with edges next to each other, with the right sides facing you. Line up the rows/stitches. Insert a tapestry needle between the first and second stitches in the first row. Slide the tapestry needle under two rows, then bring it back to the front between the first and second stitch of the row. Starting on the opposite end, work under two rows again and repeat, zig-zagging from side to side. Stitch under the strands that correspond directly to the other side without skipping rows. Keep the seam elastic by working loosely, then pulling seam stitches gently after working a few inches.

SHOULDER SEAM STITCH – STOCKINETTE

With right sides facing you, thread the yarn onto a tapestry needle. Insert the needle from back to front into the middle of the V of the first stitch on the right edge of the knitting. Pull yarn through. On the opposite side of the knitting, work from the right edge and the front side of the work. Insert the tapestry needle behind the two legs of the first stitch. Pull yarn through.

Repeat this step, inserting needle under the legs of the stitches on each side of the work. Try to match the tension of the seam to the tension of your knitting.

LONG TAIL PROVISIONAL CAST ON

There are a few different methods to create a provisional cast on, but the long tail provisional cast on is my favorite because it doesn't require a crochet hook. Using your working yarn and a piece of scrap yarn, hold both yarns together and make a slip knot. Place slip knot on your needle. Hold your yarn as you would for a long-tail cast on, but hold the working yarn over your index finger and the scrap yarn over your thumb. Cast on the number of stitches specified in the pattern, plus one stitch. Your slip knot does not count. As you cast on, you will see that your scrap yarn creates a chain at the bottom of your needle. Double check the number of cast on stitches and cut the scrap yarn. Begin working stitches with the working yarn as called for in the pattern. When you reach the slip knot, drop it and leave it as-is while you continue to knit. When you're ready to pick up the live stitches on your cast on edge, untie the slip knot and slowly unravel your scrap yarn stitches, one at a time. Use your needle to pick up each working yarn loop/stitch.

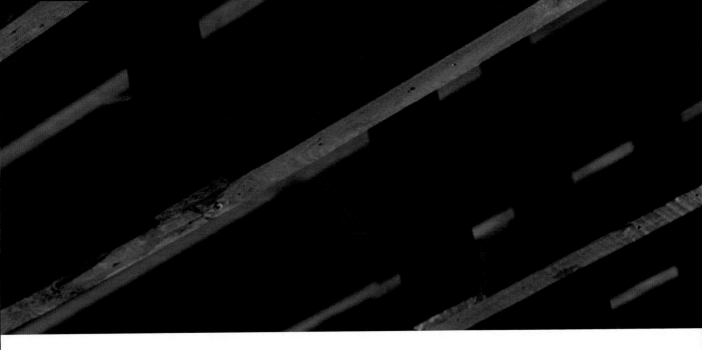

DUPLICATE STITCH

Thread scrap piece of yarn in contrasting color onto tapestry needle and decide where you want your stitching to begin. Bring the point of the tapestry needle up through the point of the V in the first stitch you want to duplicate; pull the yarn through, leaving a few inches of yarn at the back of the work to weave in later. Working from right to left, slide needle behind the V of the stitch above the stitch you are working on. Gently pull the yarn through. Next, insert the needle back through the point of the V where you started. Pull through. You have now finished one duplicate stitch. Insert the needle through point of the V in the next stitch you want to duplicate. Repeat these steps to make three decorative duplicate stitches in your contrast color. Try to keep your tension the same as the stitches you are covering. When finished, weave in loose ends, secure and cut ends.

THREE NEEDLE BIND OFF

Hold both of your needles in your left hand, keeping the right sides of knitting facing each other. Each needle should have an equal number of live stitches on it. Using a third needle with your right hand, go into the first stitch on the front needle and the first stitch on the back needle, as if to knit. Knit through both of these stitches (knitting them together) onto the needle in your right hand. Repeat once more, creating two stitches on your needle. Lift the first stitch on your right-hand needle over the second stitch and over the top of the needle, just as you would in a traditional bind off. Continue this way until you have one stitch on your right-hand needle. Cut working yarn and pull tail through last stitch to secure.

YARN FORWARD

Bring working yarn to the front of your work between the two needles, then knit next stitch specified in pattern.

KITCHENER STITCH – STOCKINETTE

Begin with the stitches to be joined on two needles held parallel to one another. (Do not bind off any of the stitches.) Using a length of matching yarn threaded onto a tapestry needle, attach the yarn at the right-hand edge of the upper/top piece. Graft the first two parallel stitches by inserting the tapestry needle into the first stitch on the front needle purlwise. Pull the yarn through, leaving the stitch on the knitting needle. Then, insert the tapestry needle knitwise into the first stitch on the back needle and pull the yarn through, leaving the stitch on the knitting needle. Continue in this manner until you reach the last two stitches. When you reach the last two stitches, insert the tapestry needle into the first stitch on the front needle knitwise and pull the yarn through, dropping the stitch from the knitting needle. Then, insert the tapestry needle purlwise into the first stitch on the back needle and pull the yarn through, dropping the stitch from the needle. Pull the yarn tight and cut end. Weave in the tail on the inside of your work.

PICKING UP STITCHES

Slide knitting needle into an existing stitch, then slide your other needle underneath (into the stitch as if to knit.) Pull the stitch through. You now have a new stitch on your needle. Repeat until you have picked up the number of stitches specified in the pattern.

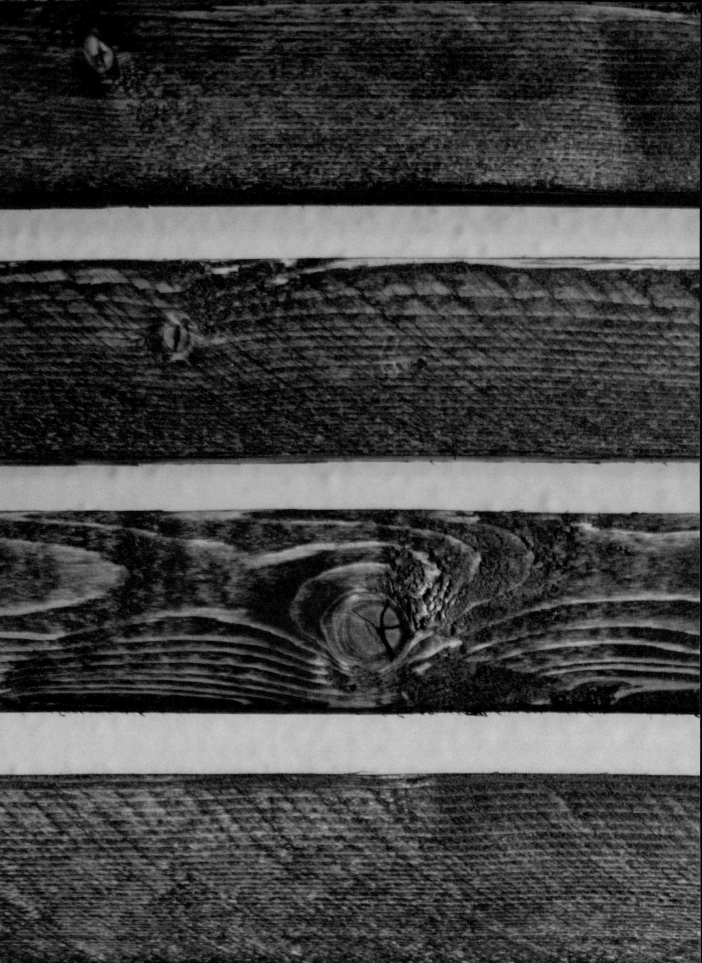

ACKNOWLEDGEMENTS

I would like to personally thank the following people for their support in the making of this book:

Stefanie Goodwin-Ritter for her top-notch technical editing skills and support in every way imaginable. You've been an invaluable source of information and resources, and I am so grateful for your patience and expertise. Above all, you've been a true friend along the way and I want to thank you for that.

Joelle Blanchard for being my behind-the-scenes everything. I had so much fun scheming and daydreaming with you. Your photography is magical and you are a beautiful person, inside and out. **Geof Fischer** for being a good friend and doing a spectacular job on both sides of the camera on a hot August day. **Joey Leaming** for jumping in and making pure magic happen, and for letting us hang out in your fantastic studio space. And **Lotus Geigley** for being the most fantastic mini-model ever. From the bottom of my heart, thank you all for making my hand-knit dreams come to life in the most beautiful way.

Erin Hogan for being there when I needed a sounding board, a live show at Wooly's, cavatelli from Orlondo's or a fantastic editor and proofreader. Thank you for being a friend.

Emily Elliott for the enthusiastic encouragement, reality checks, unending support and road-trip brainstorms. Thank you for believing in my crazy ideas when I was too chicken to tell anyone else about them.

Amy Dix and **Sarah Lacey** for giving me the gift of knitting (by teaching me how to knit). They say you never forget your first knitting mentor(s). And when your first knitting mentors are two of your closest friends, you're basically sisters for life.

My East Coast and West Coast BFFs, **Kristi Prokopiak** and **Jamaica Edgell**, who always get it. Thank you for being a huge creative force and inspiration.

Erica Carnes and **Jessica Miller** at **Hill Vintage and Knits**, my most favorite entrepreneurial yarn store owner heroes and knitXmidwest co-conspirators.

A special thank you to my local knitting friends, a gang of incredible women who I hold dear: **Sarah, Amy, Nichole, Melissa, Emily, Jenni, Alexis, Nikki, Heidi, Robyn, Olga, Angie, Darcy** and **Taylor.** We've shared so many laughs and heart-to-hearts over the years and I consider you my best of bests.

My friends at **StevenBe** for coming to the rescue in a last-minute long distance knit-mergency.

Trent Reznor, for making the absolute perfect background music for graphic design work. Your genius is the soundtrack to my life.

My heartfelt thanks to my **crafty internet friends**, far and wide, who have been there all along with support and words of encouragement via the magical world of blogs, emails, Instagram photos, Ravelry projects and Facebook groups. I love you guys.

A huge thank you to the kind people at **Rowan Yarns, Spud & Chloë, Wool and the Gang** and **Cascade Yarns.**

My **mom** and **dad**. Thank you for letting me draw in my room all day while listening to Metallica, and never discouraging me throughout my many artistic pursuits.

And last but not least, thank you to my awesomely wild and wonderful family: My husband (and best friend) **Bo**, and my sweet and extraordinary kids, **Lotus** and **Bowen**. You put the smile on my face and the beat in my heart every single day. Thanks for your patience, support, hugs and kisses. I love you guys so much.

AT A GLANCE

ATMOSPHERE
HAT
PAGE 98

FLOOR
SCARF
PAGE 100

DEBUT
KIMONO
PAGE 102

UNDONE
PULLOVER
PAGE 112

EVENFLOW
SCARF
PAGE 116

RETROGRADE
SCARF
PAGE 118

FEEDBACK
COWL
PAGE 106

DISTORTION
HAT
PAGE 108

MINNIE
HOODED SCARF
PAGE 110

LITTLE EARTHQUAKES
COWL
PAGE 120

VALHALLA
COWL
PAGE 122

SLIVER
HAT
PAGE 124

ABOUT THE AUTHOR

Jen Geigley lives and knits in Des Moines, Iowa, with her husband and two children. Known for her clean, modern designs, Jen has an appreciation for simple knits that are easy to wear. Her designs have been published in *Knit Simple Magazine, Noro Magazine, Knitsy Magazine, Love of Knitting Magazine, Rowan's Online Publications* and she has self-published knitwear patterns online since 2010. Jen is passionate about sharing her love of knitting by teaching beginner knitting classes to adults and children at local schools and workshops, and loves to knit with her daughter. Originally trained in the arts, she creates her own sketches, illustrations, schematics and graphic design work. In her spare time, she enjoys watching Quentin Tarantino movies, going to concerts and listening to alt, metal and punk rock music.

Website: www.jengeigley.com
Blog: www.heyjenrenee.com